Tao Teh King

An Ancient Therapy
The Way of Non-Directiveness

by
Alva LaSalle Kitselman

Published in the USA and the UK
by

MASTERWORKS INTERNATIONAL
27 Old Gloucester Street
London
WC1N 3XX
UK

Email: admin@mwipublishing.com
Web: http:/www.mwipublishing.com

ISBN: 978-0-9565803-9-9
copyright © A. L. Kitselman 1936, 2013

Orginally published
The School of Simplicity, Palo Alto, California
copyright 1936 by A. L. Kitselman II

Cover and internal illustrations by mywizarddesign.com
© Morag Campbell 2013

Publisher's Preface

Since their very beginnings, some 2500 or more years ago, both Taoism and Buddhism, as profound philosophies of living, have undoubtedly helped hundreds of millions of people to deal more effectively with the challenges of everyday life. However, it is only since the 1970s that their influence has really been felt in the field of counselling and psychotherapy through the creation of numerous approaches that draw quite strongly on the Buddhist philosophical tradition.

Taoism has not had the same impact on modern psychotherapeutic models. Yet, as early as 1936, Alva LaSalle Kitselman who was, at that time, studying oriental languages at Stanford University, with a particular emphasis on Sanskrit, created his own version of the classic text of the Taoist tradition - the book of Lao Tzu (Lao Tsu/Tse) entitled the *Tao Teh King (Tao Te Ching)*. He published the book under his own imprint called 'The Philosophers Press.' His version was, as he said, a restatement rather than being a new translation from the ancient Chinese. After its publication, and through a chance encounter with one of the librarians at Stanford, he began to realise that Taoism and Taoist philosophy could be used as a form of therapy, specifically in the form he called 'non-directive therapy.'

Some fifteen years later Kitselman created what he called 'The Institute of Integration,' which became one of the largest publishers of audio lectures on the subject of personal integration in existence at that time. Much of his inspiration came from the great teachers whom he referred to as 'The Time Teachers', these being the Rishi Kapila, Krishna, Lao Tzu, the Buddha and Jesus Christ. In the modern era he was also deeply interested in the teachings of Jiddu Krishnamurti. Kitselman was a contemporary and friend of Alan Watts and Paul Reps and was also a student of Nyogen Senzaki and other teachers in the Zen tradition in that same time period.

Kitselman was a highly talented mathematician and early computer programmer. His interest in mathematics had an unusual effect on his approach to 'personal integration', as he called it, in that he referred to different levels of therapeutic work on personal psychological integration by using the classification of A, B, C, D, and E therapies. Indeed, in 1952 he authored a book called simply '*E-Therapy*' which was a simple and yet profound statement of an approach to personal integration based upon listening to and connecting with the deep inner wisdom within. Essentially, it was what he called 'revery therapy' and was highly meditative in its approach. However, all this work was to come much later than his initial insight into the value and use of Taoism as a form of psychotherapy which took place 1936 when Kitselman was just twenty-two years old.

In his own words taken from an audio lecture he delivered in 1953 entitled "An Ancient Therapy," he says:

"I am going to present to you, this evening, one of the first methods of therapy that I learned. It might be described as non-directiveness itself. I'm going to read a book of mine which was published in 1936, which is long out of print. This little book is called the Tao Teh King *of Lao Tzu, who lived 600BC and was one of the world's classical authorities in the field of integration. This is not a literal translation; it is a restatement made from a number of translations. I had not then studied the original text. I haven't studied it to this day to the degree I'd like to and I would say that perhaps five to ten percent of the full meaning of the original text is available in this restatement.*

There is a forward which reads as follows:

Little is known of Lao-Tzu; only his
teaching survives.
The teaching itself is not important;
Only its application is of value.
Someday even this will be forgotten, and
only Tao will remain."

"Back in 1936 when I made this restatement of the Tao Teh King *I did not think it had much practical value except for the man who wanted to live quietly. It is quieting to the mind and I thought, well, it would be a nice way to live, so I decided I would try it for one summer. I had spent all winter living in a large house on the Stanford University campus giving symphony concerts with a large set of speakers and recordings every*

Saturday night to which a great many students came and after the concert was over there wasn't anything else they could do; they had to listen to me talk and listen to whatever I was wound up on at that time. I never aroused any genuine interest. Sometimes there would be a mild reflection of interest but never any genuine interest, so I decided that I wasn't getting anywhere in trying to influence people so I would sort of withdraw.

I moved into a small house in the centre of town this house wasn't even on the street; it was in a bungalow in the centre of the block. I moved there with my then wife and baby, in fact no, the baby was about to arrive, that was it, and this was during the summer period at Stanford when about eighty percent of all the students we knew had gone away. Well, in this little house we expected to live a very quiet life and I decided to live according to the Tao Teh King, to maintain nothing, and I thought it would give me a nice quiet life during the summer. As I mentioned, eighty percent of the students had gone. Partly on the account of the arrival of the baby, one friend of ours, a redheaded Irishman, a librarian at Stanford University, came out and made a courtesy call and while he was there he expressed something that was on his mind and I said "is that so" or "what makes you say that" and he went on and talked some more and I said, when he paused, I said "well that's interesting" "or "how do you figure?" or something of that sort. In other words, I didn't maintain anything; I didn't even maintain silence. I put in words at the right place and I took no part whatever in steering the conversation, and the result was my friend got a great deal off his chest. He was allowed to express himself. He experienced what Dr Breuer would call a catharsis, on an intellectual level, instead of having his outflow of thoughts impeded by my outflow of thoughts, why he was allowed a sort of an open range in which to speak and think and he went away thinking Kitselman was a remarkably intelligent fellow to talk to. Kitselman is a wise man because he had gained a great deal of insight during his conversation with me in which I had followed the simple rule of not maintaining anything, not taking any stand at all.

Well, strange as it may seem, before very long the librarian came back with a friend of his and they both talked to me and I used exactly the same method. I had no thought that there was anything effective about this except that it was just a way of me keeping quiet and calm, so I maintained nothing; I took no part in the conversation other than to make suitable noises during pauses. Well believe it or not, though there were no symphony concerts given, that little house, in spite of the fact that eighty percent of the students had gone away, that little house was full of people morning, noon and night for the remainder of that summer. People who would come to talk with me. In other words, the teaching which I had thought was practical only for the individual who wanted to be quiet was far more practical than my big house and my efforts to entertain and getting people interested and yet, you know, I was so stupid that it never occurred to me that that was the most important therapy.

I had a therapy at that time very much like the, 'client centred therapy' later developed by Dr Carl R. Rogers. I had it in a very easy, simple to understand form. I was helping a lot of people and I was too dumb to notice it, way back in 1936. *It's a therapy that any of you can try. Dr Rogers' therapy is more or less an attitude on your part that you are sure the individual can solve his problems; he talks about this and you kind of go along with him, "yes I see that," "do you feel that way?" and so forth; give him a little company and he will work out his problems. This method doesn't even involve the element of agreement; it's more like, "is that so?" "well how do you figure?" It's just allowing him a way of getting things clear off his chest and then there is a method somewhat related which comes from a study of Mr Krishnamurti's method and that is to ask a question which goes into more internal causes. If a man says "I don't like the political situation, it's corrupt," say not just "well what makes you think so?" but "I wonder what the cause corruption is?" - something like that. That would be more of perhaps a Krishnamurti inspired method, but methods of that sort in conversation constitute very good therapy and a study of the* Tao Teh King *in any one of its many translations will give one something of the feel of non-directiveness and this* Tao, *which is another name for E, is the most interesting thing to think about.*

I should've said at the beginning that if you kind of relax and listen to the Tao Teh King *it's a kind of therapy while you listen. I hope that a good many of you did that anyway.*

The late President (Franklin D. ed.) Roosevelt had a copy of my Tao The King *which he kept by his bed and used to read it to go to sleep at night. He got it because I happened to be acquainted with one of his brain trusters who also had the book and I had a psychiatrist friend who used to recommend it to his patients as a soporific to help them go to sleep. Well that is one quality that it does have. You ponder on the* Tao *and some of its amazing attributes, some of the mysterious statements that Lao Tzu makes and your mind is quieted; many parts of you go to sleep and rest. There are also some things in the little book, the* Tao Teh King, *that you can apply immediately, the minute you put the book down, in daily living. It's something that can be done right away; you don't have to go through any learned or elaborate process of accumulating instructions and techniques. It's an amazing therapy to have come out of China 2550 years ago, twenty five and half centuries. So I hope you have enjoyed the presentation of the* Tao Teh King *and I would appreciate hearing from any of you as to what you think about it and what you think about the method of non-directiveness as applied in conversation."*

In the penultimate paragraph above, Kitselman refers to the value of listening to the *Tao Teh King* when it is spoken aloud. Indeed, in the 1950s Kitselman's Institute of Integration published an extensive series of audio lectures on all aspects of personal integration including a series called the "Classical Authorities on Integration" in which he read out loud from various ancient texts and gave detailed commentary. He created over seven hours of lecturing on the *Tao Teh King*. These original lectures are available on the website dedicated to Kitselmans's life and work.*

It is the publisher's hope that this new edition of the *Tao Teh King,* coupled with Kitselman's unique audio commentary, will inspire a new generation of therapists to consider how this simple yet extraordinary philosophy can add a new dimension to their work.

MWI Publishing
Ireland 2013

*http://www.kitselman.com

Tao Teh King

This book is dedicated
to the Tao
whence it came

Foreword

Little is known of Lao-Tzu; only his
teaching survives.
The teaching itself is not important;
only its application is of value.
Some day even this will be forgotten,
and only Tao will remain.

It might be more accurate
to call this book

The Path of Stillness

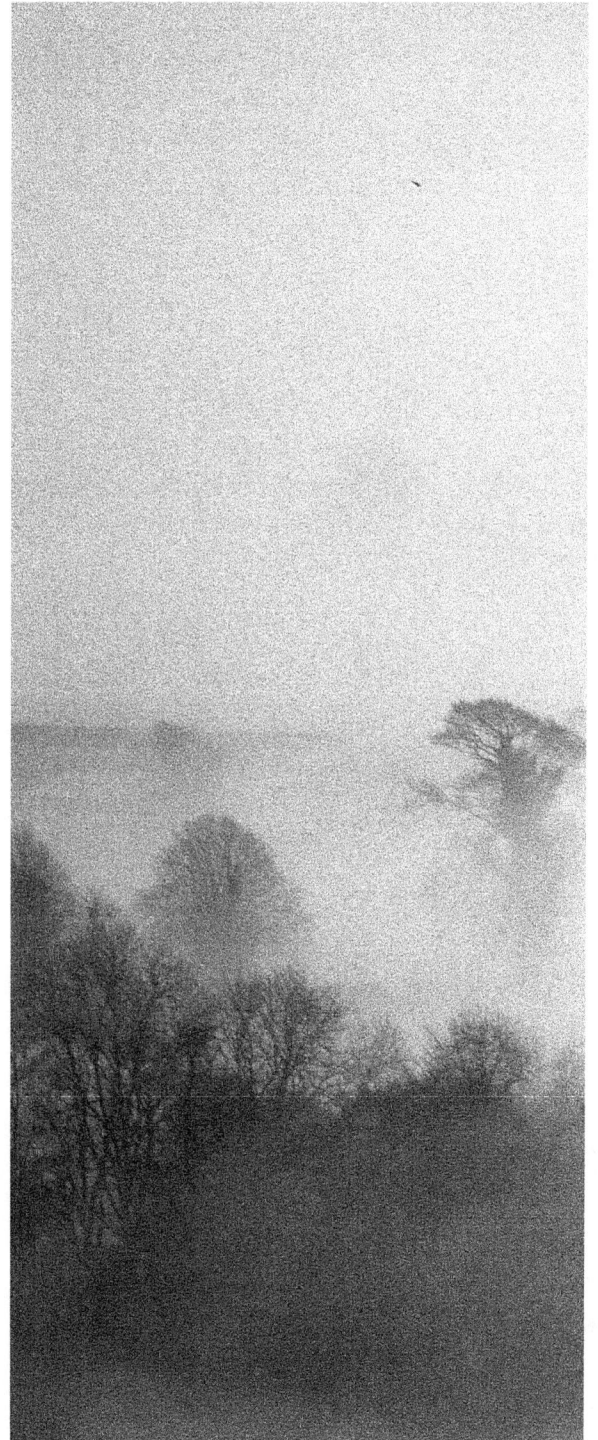

1:1   The Tao that can be known is not the changeless Tao. The name that can be spoken is not the changeless name.

1:2   When thought of as having no name, Tao is the essence of heaven and earth; when thought of as having a name, Tao is the Mother of all things.

1:3   The desireless approach the heart of Tao; the desirous reach only the surface.

1:4   Both named and nameless aspects of Tao are really the same; time and change bring different names, which, together, we call the Mystery. Where the Mystery is the deepest is the gate of all that is subtle and wonderful.

2:1　　One cannot think of beauty without knowing what ugliness is; the idea of beauty could not exist without the idea of ugliness. Similarly, the thought of skilfulness involves the thought of unskilfulness.

2:2　　So it is that opposites presuppose each other; they are coexistent, and cannot exist separately. The creation of beauty is at the same time the creation of ugliness in other things.

2:3　　Therefore, in order to avoid opposites, the sage manages his affairs without doing anything, and conveys his instructions without the use of speech.

2:4　　He causes things to happen without acting or claiming ownership or expecting reward; hence, his power is never jeopardized.

3:1 Not to reward superior ability is the way to keep the people from rivalry; not to prize things which are difficult to procure is the way to keep them from becoming thieves; not to excite their desires is the way to keep them peaceful.

3:2 Therefore the sage, in governing, calms their minds, attends to their simple needs, stills their cravings, and teaches them simplicity.

3:3 He keeps them peaceful and desireless, and keeps others who are desirous from manifesting their desires. Where there is abstinence from action, good order is universal.

4:1   Tao is like emptiness; we must guard against fullness. How deep and unfathomable Tao is, as if it were the forerunner of all things!

4:2   We should expand our beliefs and settle our differences; we should universalize our individuality and bring ourselves into agreement with others; we should cover our superiority and make ourselves appear like unto the inferior ones.

4:3   How pure and still the Tao is, as if it were eternally changeless! I do not know whence it came. perhaps it existed before all other things.

5:1   Heaven and earth do not act from any wish to be benevolent; they deal with all things according to their nature. Likewise the sage does not act from any wish to be benevolent; he deals with people according to their nature.

5:2   Much speech leads to swift exhaustion; save your thoughts and keep them free.

6:1   The Tao never dies, always changeless; it is the root of all things. when used gently and without the touch of pain, its power remains long.

7:1   Heaven and earth are long enduring because they do not live for themselves.

7:2   Therefore the sage puts his own person last, and yet it is found in the foremost place; he treats his person as if it were foreign to him, and yet that person is preserved. Is it not because he has no personal or private ends that therefore such ends are realized?

8:1   The highest excellence is like water,
which benefits all things and yet occupies
without striving the low place which all
men dislike. Therefore it is near to the Tao.

8:2   The excellence of a residence is in its
location; that of the mind is in abysmal
stillness; that of associations is in their
being with the virtuous; that of
government is in securing good order;
that of action is in effectiveness; and
that of a movement is in its timeliness.

8:3   When one maintains nothing, no one finds
fault with him.

9:1 The empty vessel is most easily carried. The sharpest point is easily dulled if often felt.

9:2 Material luxuries must always be guarded, and sometimes lead to arrogance, which brings more evil on itself. When the work is done and one's name is becoming distinguished, to withdraw into obscurity is the way of the sage.

10:1   When the body and ego are held together in one embrace they can be kept from separating. When one gives undivided attention to the breath and brings it under the utmost degree of control he can become pliant as a child. When one has cleansed away the most tempting sights and thoughts one can become perfect.

10:2   In loving the people and ruling the state, cannot the sage proceed without any action? While his intelligence reaches in every direction, cannot he be without knowledge?

10:3   He can produce and nourish without claiming anything as his own. he can do anything without anyone being aware of it. He can preside over all, and yet without controlling. this is the Mysterious Quality.

11:1 The many spokes unite in one hub; but it is on the empty center that the use of the wheel depends. The usefulness of a vessel is in its hollowness. The usefulness of a room depends upon the space within it. Therefore that which has a material existence serves for profitable adaptation, and that which has no material existence is the truly useful.

12:1   Color deprives the eyes of sight; sound makes deaf the ears; flavor deprives the mouth of taste; excitement drives the mind mad; the search for rarities causes evil conduct.

12:2   Therefore the sage seeks to satisfy the belly and not the senses. He renounces sense pleasures, preferring only to keep his person in good condition.

13:1   Favor and disgrace should be feared equally, and honor and calamity are merely personal conditions.

13:2   Disgrace is the result of loss of favor; favor always involves fear of disgrace. Honor and calamity are personal conditions because they depend on having the body. What honor or calamity could come to me if I had not the body?

13:3   Therefore he who regards the universe as his body and loves everything in it as he loves his own body is the man to be entrusted with government, for he is uninfluenced by favor or disgrace and unafraid of honor or calamity.

14:1   That which we cannot see we call the invisible; that which we cannot hear we call the inaudible; that which we cannot touch we call the intangible: that which possesses all of these three qualities we call the indescribable unity.

14:2   It cannot be discussed in terms of opposites. it is nameless, changeless, and inexpressible. This is the form of the formless, the appearance of the invisible, the feel of the intangible, the sound of the inaudible. This is the description of the indescribable.

14:3   He who has perceived this indescribable unity without attributes has learned the secret of the Tao.

15:1 The skilful masters of olden times, with subtle and exquisite penetration learned this secret and like it were incomprehensible to men. Since they were thus beyond human description, I shall try to describe their appearance.

15:2 Shrinking they seemed like those afraid of the cold in winter; undecided as though fearful of all around them; grave as though in awe of everything; fugitive like melting ice; unpretentious as a post; empty like a desert; and dull like muddy water.

15:3 How can muddy water be made clear? Let it be still and gradually it will become clear. How can motion be stopped? Let it go on and gradually it will stop.

15:4 It is because they who preserve this method of the Tao do not wish to be saturated with ego that they prefer to seem worn and not appear new and complete.

16:1 Emptiness should be developed to the utmost degree and stillness should be guarded with unwearying vigor. All things go through their processes of activity and then return whence they came. This returning is to the state of stillness; therefore stillness may be regarded as a sign of completion.

16:2 This return to stillness is an invariable rule. To know that in stillness lies achievement is to be intelligent; not to know leads to trouble and confusion. The knowledge of this invariable rule produces great sympathy and understanding, and these lead to a realization of the unity of all things. From this feeling of unity comes kingliness of character, and he who is kinglike goes on to be heavenlike. In this likeness to heaven he possesses the Tao, and possessed of the Tao he endures long. To the end of his bodily life he is exempt from all danger of decay.

17:1   At first such men were unknown; in the next age they were loved and praised; in the next they were feared; and in the next they were despised. When the pillars of faith are deficient, a want of faith ensues.

17:2   How undecided did the ancient masters appear, deeming it unwise to speak! Their work was accomplished and their undertakings were successful. While the people thought themselves to be the doers.

18:1   When the great Tao was no longer sought,
benevolence and righteousness came into
fashion. cleverness and shrewdness
appeared, and great hypocrisy followed.

18:2   When harmony was lost and malcontents
had brought disorder, sages appeared
and said,

19:1   "It would be much better for the people if we could renounce our cleverness and discard our shrewdness. Once more would they be loving and kindly if we could give up benevolence and righteousness. No more would there be thieves or robbers if we could stop our scheming and discard our wealth."

19:2   But worldly minds thought olden ways lacked elegance, and sought to ridicule the sages. However, simple views and courses plain and true have beaten many arguments.

20:1 When we renounce learning we have no trouble. there is a world of difference between the assent of the willing and that of the flatterer, though perhaps they sound alike. What all men fear is indeed to be feared, but how wide and without end is the range of questions!

20:2 The multitude of men look satisfied and pleased; I alone seem listless and still, my desires having as yet given no indication of their presence. I am like an infant that has not yet smiled. I look dejected and forlorn as if I were without a home. The multitude of men appear to have plenty; I seem to have lost everything. I seem to be a stupid man in a state of chaos. ordinary men look bright and intelligent. While I seem to be benighted. they look full of discrimination while I alone appear dull and confused. I seem to be carried about as on the sea, drifting as if I had nowhere to rest. All men have their spheres of action, while I seem dull and incapable like a simple bumpkin. I alone am different from other men, for I value the Tao.

21:1   The grandest of our earthly sights finds birth in Tao, the invisible and indescribable. All forms are hidden in its formlessness; all sights in its invisibility; all motion in its changelessness. so it is that all things return unto the Tao, and therefore never know decay. This is a truth because

22:1   The unassuming become accomplished; the empty become full. He who concentrates attains; he whose desires are many does not realize them.

22:2   Therefore the sage holds in his embrace the unity of all things and manifests it to all the world. He is free from selfdisplay, and therefore shines; free from selfassertion, and therefore is distinguished; free from self-praise, and therefore is considered meritorious; free from self-satisfaction, and therefore becomes superior. Because he does not strive, no one can strive with him.

22:3   The saying of the ancients that the "partial becomes complete" was not vainly spoken; all real completion is comprehended in it.

23:1 He who abstains from speech understands his own nature. Violent winds and sudden rains do not last long. If heaven and earth cannot make such utterances lengthy, how much less can man!

23:2 When one is making the Tao his business those who are also pursuing it agree with him in it. Those who are making the manifestation of its course their object

21:1 agree with him in that, and even those who are failing in both these things agree with him where they fail.

23:3 Hence those with whom he agrees as to

22:1 the Tao, those with whom he agrees as to its manifestation, and those with whom he agrees in their failure all have the

22:2 happiness of understanding and sympathy. But when there is not sufficient faith, a want of faith ensues.

24:1 He who stands on his tiptoes does not stand firm; he who stretches his legs does not walk; he who displays himself does not shine; he who asserts his views is not distinguished; he who praises himself does not find his merit acknowledged; he who is self-conceited has no superiority allotted to him. Such conditions when viewed from the standpoint of the Tao are like disfigurements which all dislike; hence those who seek the Tao do not adopt or allow them.

25:1   Something complete and undefiled came into existence before heaven and earth. It was still and formless, alone and changeless, omnipresent and untouched. It is the source of all things.

25:2   I do not know its name, and I give it the designation of the Tao. Trying further to give it a name, I call it the immeasurable.

25:3   Immeasurable, it extends everywhere: it is both remote and nearby. Therefore the Tao is immeasurable; heaven is immeasurable; earth is immeasurable; and the sage is also immeasurable. In the universe these four are immeasurable, and the sage is one of them.

25:4   Man takes his law from the earth; earth takes its law from heaven; heaven takes its law from the Tao. The law of the Tao is its own nature.

26:1   Gravity is the root of lightness; stillness is the ruler of movement. Therefore the wise prince maintains his stillness and gravity. Light actions or too much activity will cost him his throne.

27:1   The skilful traveller leaves no traces; the skilful speaker says nothing offensive; the skilful calculator does not count. In the same way the sage, being skilful at saving men, excludes none; being skilful at saving things, does not cast anything away. This is called proceeding without traces.

27:2   Therefore the skilful man is the master of the unskilful man; and the unskilful man is the helper of the skilful man. If the helper did not honor the master and the master did not rejoice in the helper, they might greatly err. This is a complementary form of the unity of all things.

28:1	The highest excellence lies in non-indulgence.
28:2	The sage advocates no measures of limitation.
29:1	He who desires the kingdom for himself will never gain it.
29:2	Hence the sage renounces all action and desire.
30:1	Arms beget arms.
30:2	Bad years follow great armies.

30:3   A skilful one strikes a decisive blow and then stops, not daring to assert and complete his mastery. Guarding against boastfulness and arrogance, He strikes only because of necessity and not because of a desire for mastery.

30:4   Things which attain maturity become old and are ended, for it is not in accordance with the Tao to attain maturity.

31:1 The use of arms is not in accordance with the Tao.

31:2 He who delights in the slaughter of men cannot get his will in the kingdom, and all who advocate the use of arms are such.

31:3 He who has killed multitudes of men should weep for them with the bitterest grief, and the victor in battle has his place accordingly.

32:1   When thought of as changeless, the Tao has no name.

32:2   It has power over all things.

32:3   It is all-pervading.

32:4   Whenever it assumes form it can be named and understood. Those who understand it are free from all risk of failure and error.

32:5   Tao is to all the world as a great river is to all its tributary streams.

33:1 He who knows other men is discerning; he who knows himself is intelligent. He who overcomes others is strong; he who overcomes himself is mighty. He who is satisfied with his lot is rich; he who perseveres in the Tao is richest.

33:2 He who lives up to the requirements of his position continues long in it; he who renounces life and yet does not perish has longevity.

34:1   All-pervading is Tao the immeasurable.

34:2   It gives rise to all things without display. It may be found in the smallest things and in the greatest things.

34:3   Thus the sage is able to accomplish his great achievements. By not making himself great he becomes great.

35:1   The whole world goes to him who knows
the secret of the Tao. He gives peace and
rest to all.

35:2   The pleasures of the senses may at first
seem more appealing than the Tao. But the
Tao is inexhaustible.

36:1   All things may be controlled by their opposites, upon which they depend. this is the secret method.

36:2   The soft overcomes the hard; and the weak the strong.

36:3   No disturbance should be brought about; instruments for the good of all should not be trusted to individuals.

37:1   The Tao does no one thing; therefore it does all things.

37:2   All things are of themselves transformed by one who knows the Tao.

37:3   It is the nameless simplicity that brings universal order and peace.

38:1   Those who do not manifest their understanding of the Tao understand it in the highest degree; those who take pains to keep their understanding of the Tao understand it in a lesser degree.

38:2   Those who do nothing and have no need of doing anything possess the Tao in the highest degree; those who do things and have need of doing things possess the Tao in a lesser degree.

38:3   Those possessed of the highest benevolence are always seeking to carry it out and have no need to be doing so, as also are those possessed of the highest righteousness.

38:4   Those possessed of the highest propriety are always showing it, and if men do not respond, They bare the arm and march upon them.

38:5   So it is that when the Tao is lost its attributes appear; when the attributes are lost benevolence appears; when benevolence is lost righteousness appears; and when righteousness is lost propriety appears.

38:6   Propriety is the attenuated form of loyalty and good faith, and is also the commencement of disorder. It is only a by-product of the Tao and is the beginning of stupidity.

38:7   Therefore the sage seeks the Tao itself and not its attributes.

39:1   All things are manifestations of the unity of all things.

39:2   If this unity did not exist great breaks would occur and harmony would be lost.

39:3   Thus the greatest dignity is based upon humility and sympathy toward all.

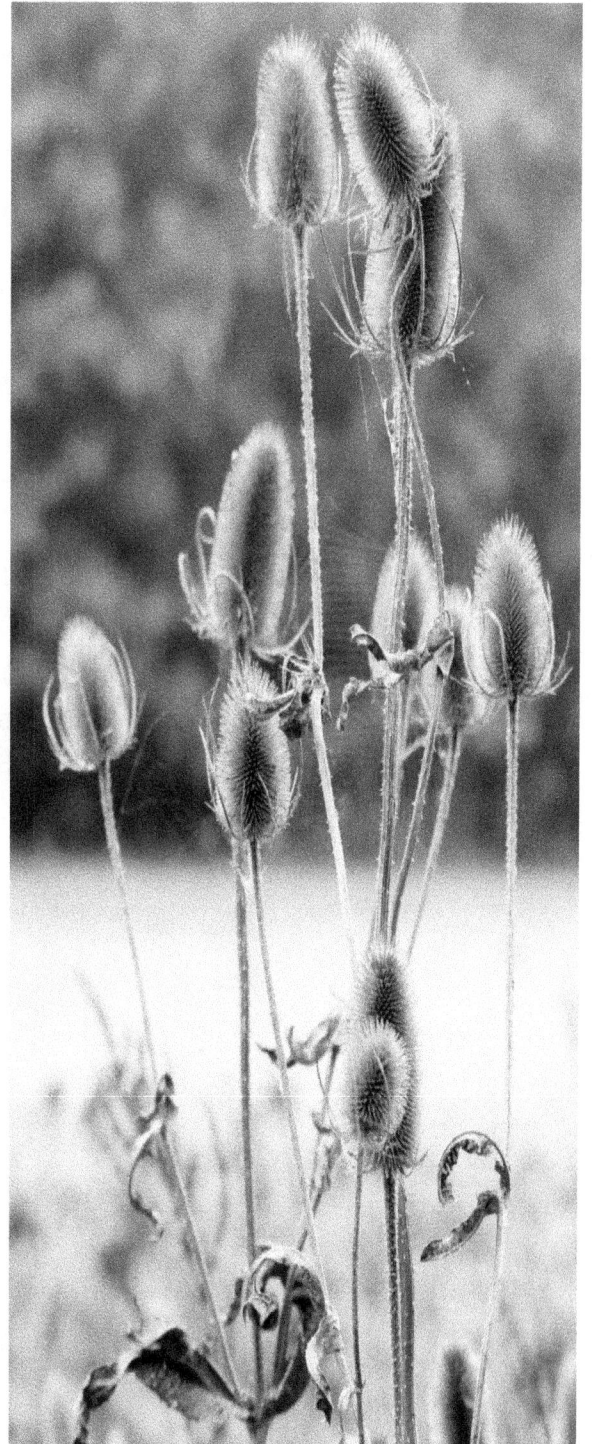

40:1   Tao manifests itself in opposites. Its mightiest works are done without display of force.

40:2   All things sprang from the existing Tao; the existing Tao sprang from the Tao that does not exist.

41:1　Scholars of the highest class earnestly carry the Tao into practice. Scholars of the middle class seem now to keep it and now to lose it. Scholars of the lowest class laugh greatly at it. if it were not thus laughed at. it would not be fit to be the Tao.

41:2　It is because of this that word-flingers scoff at the Tao.

41:3　The Tao is hidden and has no name; but it is the Tao that is skilful at giving and making complete.

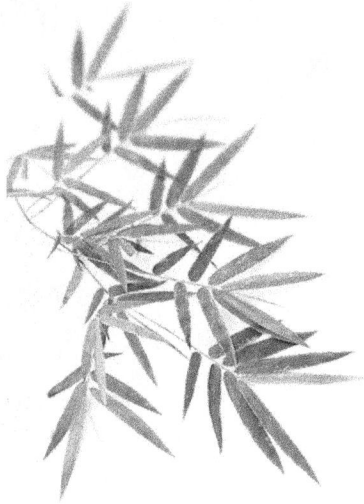

42:1 The Tao produced unity; unity produced duality; duality produced multiplicity; and so all things came to be.

42:2 Men dislike to be lowly, and yet the greatest have styled themselves thus. So it is that some things are increased by being diminished, and other things are diminished by being increased.

42:3 What other men teach I also teach. The violent and strong do not die their natural death. I will make this the basis of my teaching.

43:1   The softest thing in the world dashes against and overcomes the hardest; that which has no material existence enters where there is no crevice. By this I know what advantage belongs to doing nothing.

43:2   Few attain to this understanding without the use of words.

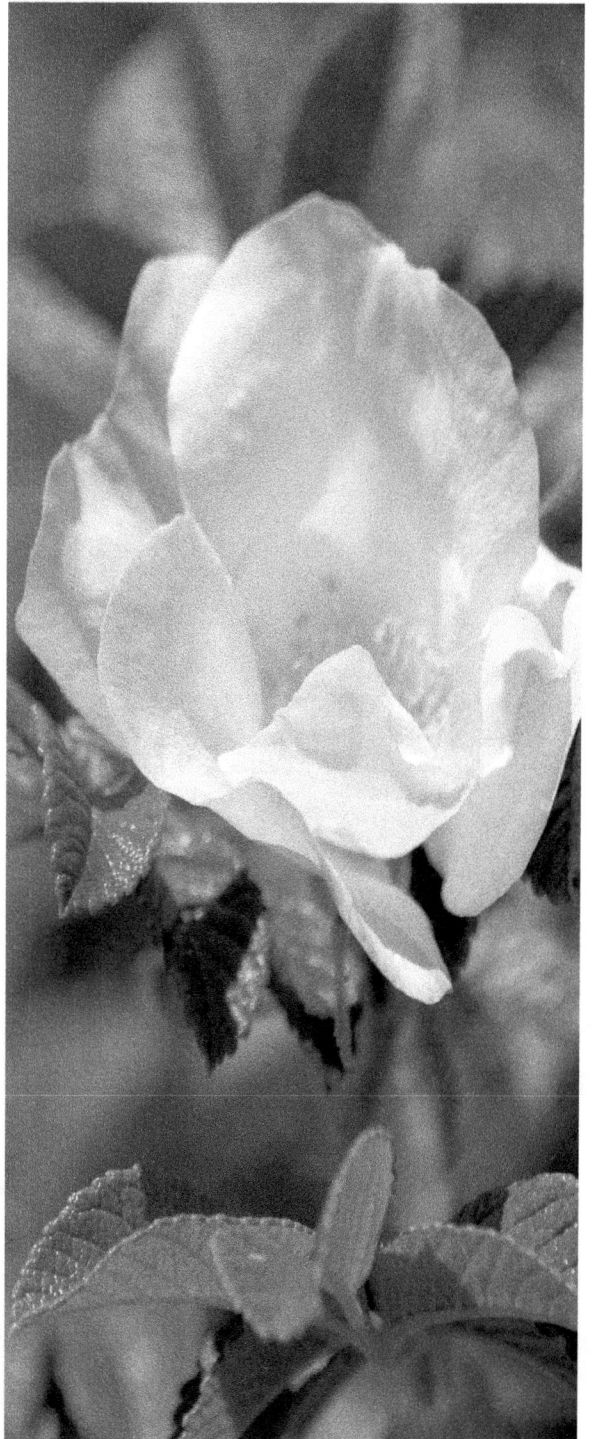

44:1   Do you prefer fame to life? or wealth to life?

44:2   So we see that life is worth more than fame or wealth.

44:3   He who is truly content fears nothing; he who is truly blameless does nothing.
                          Long shall he live.

45:1   He excels who regards his best
achievements as inconsequential.

45:2   Action overcomes cold;
stillness overcomes heat.
The value of stillness is the
universal law.

46:1 When the Tao prevails, peace prevails. when the Tao is disregarded, strife results.

46:2 There is no guilt greater than to sanction ambition; no calamity greater than to be discontented with ones lot; no fault greater than the wish to acquire. Therefore a sufficiency of contentment is an enduring and unchanging sufficiency.

47:1 Without going outside his door a man can be aware of everything that happens; without looking out of his window he can see the Tao of all things. The farther one travels the less he knows.

47:2 Therefore the sages secured their knowledge without travelling; understood things without seeing them; and accomplished their ends without any purpose of doing so.

48:1   He who devotes himself to learning seeks from day to day to increase; he who devotes himself to the Tao seeks from day to day to diminish.

48:2   He diminishes himself continually until he arrives at the state of doing nothing. Having arrived at this state, there is nothing which he does not do.

48:3   He who would gain heaven and earth should do so by taking no trouble about it. He who troubles himself is not sufficient to gain heaven and earth.

49:1   The sage has no mind of his own; the mind of the people is his mind.

49:2   To those who are good I am good, and to those who are not good I am also good; thus goodness is made to grow. To those who are sincere I am sincere, and to those who are not sincere I am also sincere; thus sincerity is made to grow.

49:3   The sage has in the world an appearance of indecision and keeps his mind in a state of indifference to all. The people keep their eyes and ears directed to him and he deals with them all as his children.

50:1   Men enter life and return from it to whence they came.

50:2   Of every ten, three bring life and three bring death.

50:3   There are also three in every ten who wish for life but who cause death instead because they try too hard to perpetuate life.

50:4   But there is one who is skilful in managing the life entrusted to him. He endures long and cannot be injured in any way, because there is in him no place of death.

51:1 All things are produced and nourished by the Tao. They receive their forms according to their various natures, and are completed according to their surroundings. Therefore all things without exception honor the Tao and exalt its manifestations.

51:2 This honoring of the Tao and exalting of its manifestations is not the result of any ruling but is always a spontaneous tribute.

51:3 Thus the Tao causes all things.

51:4 Its operation in this respect is called mysterious because it does so invisibly, inaudibly, and intangibly.

52:1   The Tao is the origin of all things.

52:2   In knowing the Tao we know its manifestations. He who guards that of the Tao that is within him will be free from peril to the end of his life.

52:3   Let him be silent and renounce his senses and all his life he will be exempt from difficulty; let him talk and seek to satisfy his senses and all his life there will be no rest for him.

52:4   The perception of the subtle is clear-sightedness; the guarding of the fine is strength.

53:1   If I were suddenly to become famous and yet still wish to live according to the Tao, what I should be most afraid of would be a boastful display.

53:2   The path of the Tao is level and even, but people love the by-paths.

53:3   They exalt that which they prefer at the expense of that which they do not prefer; this is contrary to the Tao.

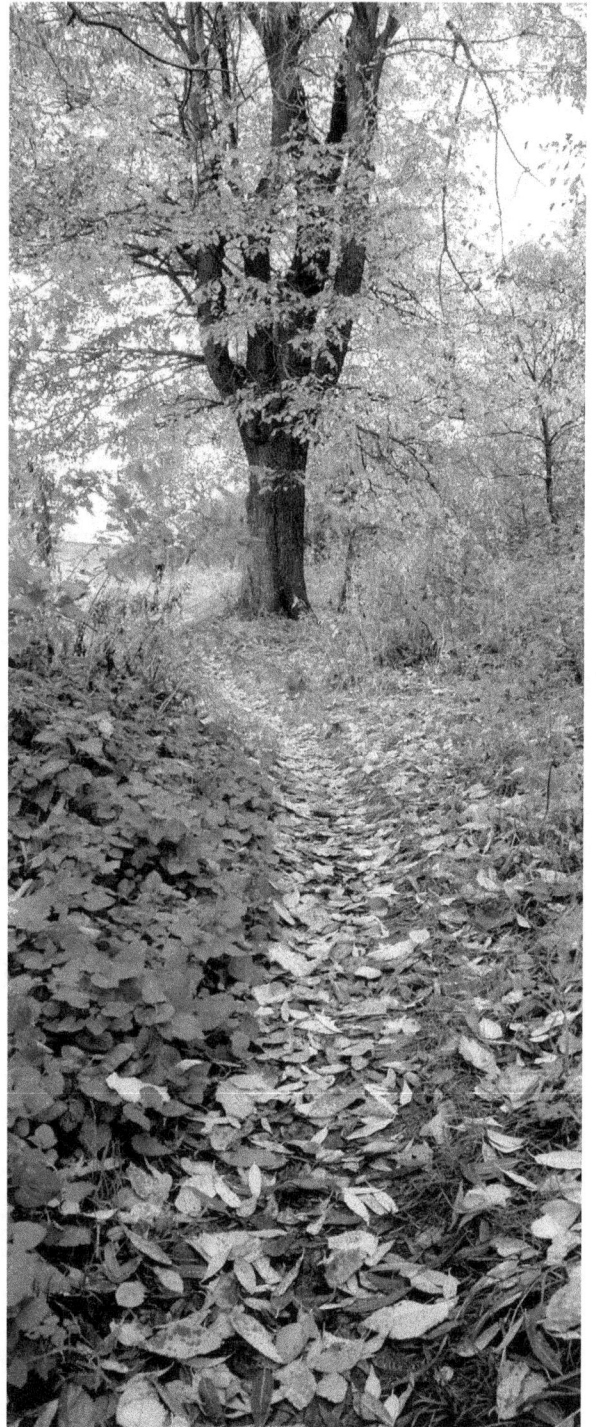

54:1   The Tao is invincible.

54:2   Its use will benefit all things.

54:3   Its effect may be seen in the individual, in the family, in the neighborhood, in the state, and in the empire. This effect of the Tao is demonstrated by the fact that

55:1   He who possesses the Tao in a high degree is like a child; no danger exists for him.

55:2   The infant is immature and yet complete, growing and yet perfect, ignorant and yet stainless, weak and yet without fatigue.

55:3   He who becomes like unto this knows the secret of the Tao. He knows the wisdom of avoiding all life-increasing arts, and the strength that lies in controlling with the mind the vital breath.

55:4   That which becomes mature and strong soon grows old, and this is contrary to the Tao. Whatever is contrary to the Tao soon ends.

56:1   He who knows speaks not; he who speaks knows not.

56:2 Be silent and renounce the senses; settle your differences and seek simplicity; seek not to shine but be in harmony with others. This is the Mysterious Agreement.

56:3   Such a person cannot be treated familiarly or distantly; he is beyond all consideration of profit or injury; of honor or misfortune: he is the noblest man under heaven.

57:1　A state may be ruled by correction; arms may be used with skill and cleverness; but the kingdom is made ones own only by freedom from action and purpose.

57:2　This is so because the multiplication of prohibitive enactments increases the poverty of the people; the more implements that add to their profit the greater disorder among the people; the more acts of crafty dexterity that men possess, the more do strange contrivances appear; the more display there is of legislation the more thieves and robbers there are.

57:3　Therefore a sage has said, "I will do nothing, and the people will be transformed of themselves; I will be fond of keeping still and the people will of themselves become correct. I will take no trouble about it and the people will of themselves become rich; I will manifest no ambition and the people will of themselves attain to the primitive simplicity."

58:1 The government which seems the most incompetent may often bring the most good; the government which deals with everything accomplishes but little. Joy and sorrow are found side by side: who knows what either will come to in the end?

58:2 Correction easily becomes distortion and the good in it easily becomes evil. Many people have been deluded on this point for a long time.

58:3 Therefore the sage makes no rulings and all things become peaceful of themselves.

59:1   For regulating the human side of our nature and rendering proper service to the heavenly side there is nothing like moderation.

59:2   It is only by moderation that an early return to stillness is affected. This early return to stillness is what I call the repeated accumulation of the attributes of Tao, and from this accumulation comes control. We do not know the limits of this control, and when one does not know what the limits shall be, he may be the ruler of a state.

59:3   He who possesses the power behind nature may continue long, because his root is deep and firm.

60:1   Governing a state is like cooking a small
fish; it must be done gently.

60:2   If the kingdom is governed according to
the Tao the spirits of the departed will be
as peaceful as are the people, and will
molest no one, for they too are governed
by the Tao.

60:3   When this harmony prevails between the
living and the departed, their good
influences are combined.

61:1   What makes a great state is its being lowly and humble; it becomes the center toward which all things under heaven flow.

61:2   We see this even in sex relations; the female always overcomes the male by her stillness, which may be considered a sort of humility.

61:3   Thus it is that a great state by condescending to small states gains them for itself; and that small states by abasing themselves to a great state win it over to them. In the one case the abasement leads to gaining adherence; in the other case to procuring favor.

61:4   The great state only wishes to unite men together and nourish them; the small state only wishes to be received by and to serve the other. Each gets what it desires, but the great state must learn to abase itself.

62:1   Tao is the greatest of all

62:2   Admirable words can purchase honor;
admirable deeds can raise their performer
above others. Even men who are not good
are not without hope.

62:3 Even a valuable presented by the ministers
of a mighty prince would not be equal in
value to a lesson of the Tao which might be
presented on bended knees.

62:4 The ancients sought Tao because it was the
only permanent thing which could be
obtained, and because it replaced guilt
with good. For this reason all under
heaven consider it to be the most
valuable of all things.

63:1   Achieve without acting; conduct affairs without effort; taste without being aware of flavor; consider the small to be great and the few to be many; repay injury with kindness.

63:2   Anticipate things that will become difficult while they are easy, and do things that will become great while they are small. All difficult things in the world are sure to arise from a previous state in which they were easy, and all great things from a state in which they were small; therefore the sage, while he never does what is great, is able in this way to accomplish the greatest things.

63:3   He who lightly promises is sure to keep but little faith; he who is continually thinking things easy is sure to find them difficult. Therefore the sage sees difficulty even in what seems easy, and so never has any difficulties.

64:1　That which is at rest is easily held; before a thing has given indications of its presence it is easy to take measures against it; that which is very small is easily dispersed. Action should be taken before a thing has made its appearance; order should be secured before disorder has begun.

64:2　All great things have small beginnings.

64:3　He who acts does harm; he who takes hold of a thing loses his hold. The sage does not act and therefore does no harm; he does not lay hold and therefore does not lose his hold. People are constantly ruining their affairs when they are on the eve of success. If they were as careful at the end as they were at the beginning they would not so ruin them.

64:4　Therefore the sage desires that which is not desired and does not prize things difficult to get; he learns what is not learned and turns back to what the multitude of men have passed by. Thus he helps the natural development of all things without daring to act.

65:1 The ancients who showed their skill in practicing the Tao did so not to enlighten the people but rather to make them simple and ignorant.

65:2 The difficulty in governing the people comes from their having much knowledge. He who governs a state by his learning is a scourge to it, while he who does not do so is a blessing.

65:3 He who knows these two things finds in them his model of behavior, and possesses the mysterious excellence. This excellence is deep and far-reaching, showing its possessor to be different from others but leading them to a great belief in him.

66:1 Rivers and seas receive the tribute of all the valley streams because they are more lowly; because of this they are the ruling bodies of water. Therefore the sage in order to be above men puts himself by his words below them, and in order to be before them places his person behind them.

66:2 In this way though he has his place above them, men do not feel his weight; though he has his place before them they do not feel it as an injury to them.

66:3 Therefore all in the world delight to exalt him and do not weary of him. Because he does not strive, no one can strive with him.

67:1   All the world bears witness to the greatness of the Tao, yet it appears to be inferior. Now it is just its greatness that makes it seem to be inferior. If it were like anything else, long would its smallness have been known.

67:2   I have three precious things which I prize and hold fast: the first is gentleness; the second is economy; and the third is humility.

67:3   With gentleness I can be bold; with economy I can be liberal; with humility I can be honorable. nowadays people give up gentleness and are all for being bold; economy, and are all for being liberal; humility, and are all for being honorable: the end of all which is death.

67:4   Gentleness is sure to be victorious, even in battle, and firmly will it maintain its ground. Heaven will save its possessor, by his very gentleness protecting him.

68:1 The warrior with the greatest skill does not resort to strife; he who fights with peace and good will never feels rage. He who continues to conquer does not approach the enemy; and he whose word men strive to hear leads a humble life.

69:1   A master of the art of war has said, "I do not wish to start a war, but only to defend; I would rather retreat than advance." This is one of the great secrets of the art of war.

69:2   There is no calamity greater than lightly engaging in war, for to do that is to lose life which is so precious. Thus it is that when weapons are crossed he who deplores conquers.

70:1   My words are very easy to understand
and very easy to practice; but there is
no one in the world who is able to
understand and practice them.

70:2   There is a compelling force of truth behind
my words and I speak the law of the
universe. It is because men do not know
these that they know me not.

70:3   I am to be prized because few comprehend
me. The sage, while outwardly appearing
poor, carries treasure in his heart.

71:1　It is highest to know and yet think we do not know; it is a disease not to know and yet to think we do know.

71:2　It is the pain of this disease that cures us of it. The sage does not have the disease because he knows the pain that is inseparable from it.

72:1　When the people do not fear what they ought to fear, that which they do fear will come upon them.

72:2　If they would not feel weary of the world, let them not indulge themselves in their ordinary life.

72:3　It is by avoiding such indulgence that such weariness does not arise.

72:4　Therefore the sage understands his own nature but does not indulge it; he is moderate in all things so that he may not weary of the world.

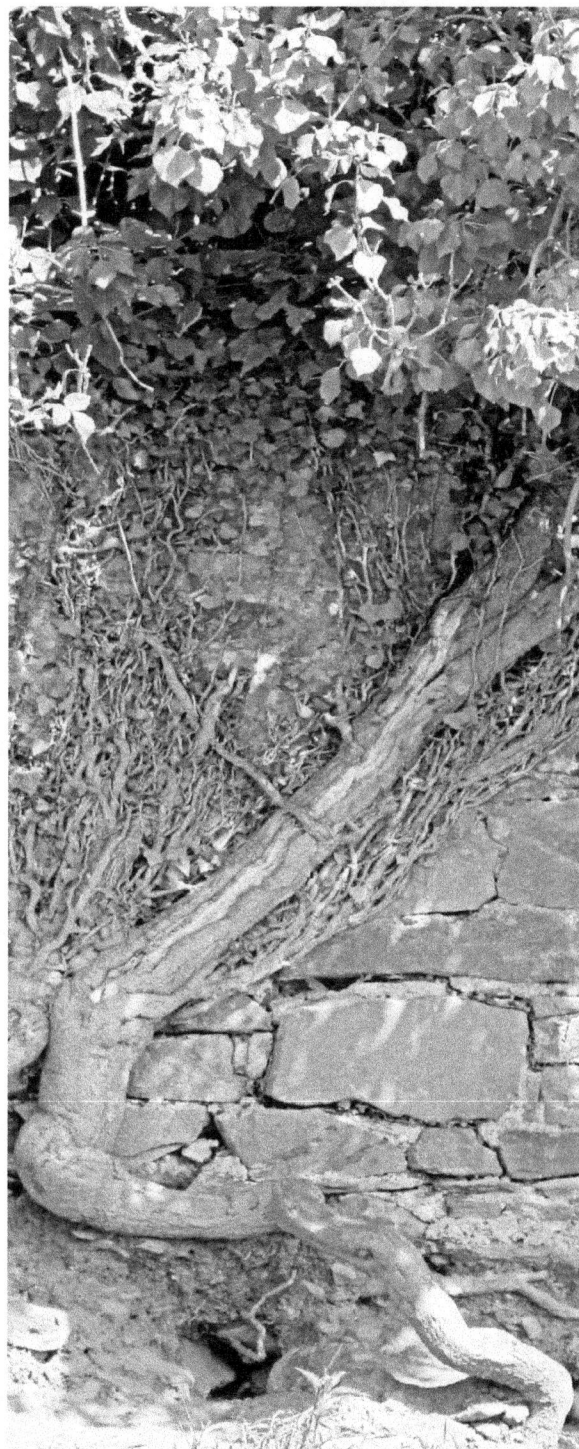

73:1 He whose boldness appears in daring is put to death; he whose boldness appears in not daring lives on. One of these cases appears to be advantageous and the other to be injurious, but the sage does not attempt to judge, for

73:2 It is not meet for man to judge in matters which heaven will decide. A mans own nature is his punishment; no one can escape.

74:1   The people do not fear death, for the death penalty does not remove crime. Therefore why try to frighten them with it?

74:2   He who would inflict death in the place of the true bringer of death is like one who hews wood in the place of a great carpenter; seldom is it that he does not cut his hands!

75:1   The people suffer from famine because of the multitude of taxes consumed by their superiors.

75:2   The people are difficult to govern because their superiors do not know how to govern them.

75:3   The people think little of dying because of the poorness and extreme difficulty of their living. Therefore if the rulers will make the life of the people pleasant there will be few who risk their lives.

76:1   Man at his birth is pliant and weak; at death he is firm and strong. So it is with all things. Trees at first are soft and weak; at death they are dry and hard.

76:2   Thus it is that firmness and strength are the companions of death; softness and weakness are the companions of life.

76:3   He who relies on his strength does not conquer; the tree which is strong is soon felled.

76:4   Therefore that which is soft and weak is superior to that which is firm and strong.

77:1 The way of the Tao lies in evenness, decreasing excesses and increasing deficiencies.

77:2 The way of man is to take away from those who have not enough and add to his own superabundance.

77:3 Only he who is in possession of the Tao can take his own superabundance and therewith serve all under heaven.

77:4 Therefore the sage acts without claiming results; he achieves without pride because he does not wish to display his superiority.

78:1   There is nothing in the world more soft
and weak than water, and yet it is
greatest in destroying the firm
and strong.

78:2   Everyone in the world knows that the
soft overcomes the hard, and the weak
the strong, but no one is able to put it
into practice.

78:3   Therefore he who accepts responsibility
for the errors of a state is regarded as
its noblest leader; he who accepts all
mens blame becomes a king.

78:4   Words that are strictly true always
seem paradoxical.

79:1   When a reconciliation is effected after a great animosity there is sure to be a grudge remaining, and this is not beneficial.

79:2   Therefore the sage keeps his part of an agreement but does not concern himself with the other persons part. He who knows the Tao thinks only of the agreement while he who does not know the Tao thinks only of his side of it.

79:3   The Tao is always on the side of the man who knows it best.

80:1   In a little state with a small population I would so order it that men with great ability would not displace other men; I would try to make the life of the people peaceful.

80:2   I should see to it that they would have no occasion to use even the luxuries that they already possess.

80:3   I would try to make them return to simple ways.

80:4   I would try to help them find luxury in a simple life.

80:5   There should be a neighboring state within sight, and the sound of its commotion and disorder should be heard all the way from it to us, but I would not permit my people to visit it or indulge their curiosity concerning it.

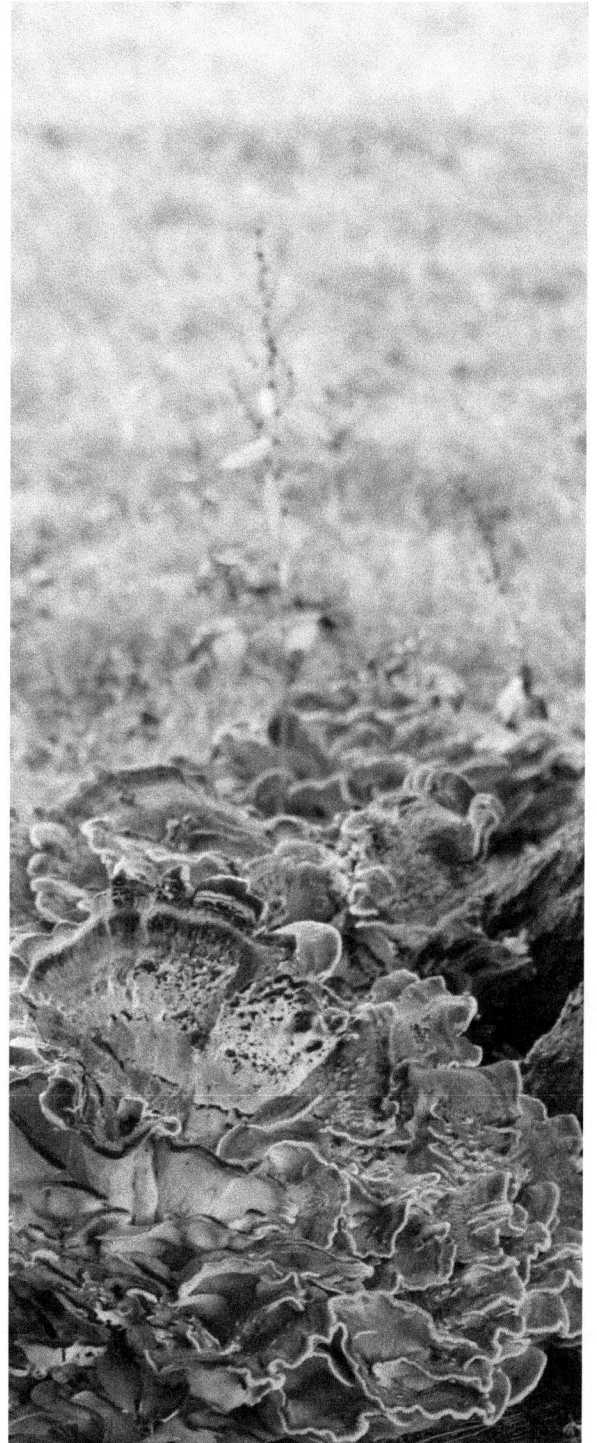

81:1   Sincere words are not fine; fine words are not sincere. those who are skilled do not dispute; the disputatious are not skilled. Those who know are not extensively learned; the extensively learned do not know.

81:2   The sage does not accumulate. The more that he expends for others the more does he possess of his own; the more he gives to others the more does he have himself.

81:3   With all the sharpness in the way of the Tao, it injures not; with all the doing in the way of the sage, he does not strive.

LAO - T Z U

A short biography
by

A. L. KITSELMAN II

The Old Philosopher

In ancient China
many sages lived
they talked and talked and talked and
talked
but Lao was silent
for Tao is silent

China had
many heroes
they fought and fought and fought and
fought
but Lao was still
for Tao is still

in old Cathay
there were great kings
they built and built and built and built
but not Lao
master of Tao

The sages, kings, and heroes
moulder in their graves
but not Lao
he is the Tao

He never changes

Visit

www.kitsleman.com

for details on other material by A. L. Kitsleman as well as further biographical information. The website also offerns many of Kitselman's original audio recordings.

E-Therapy

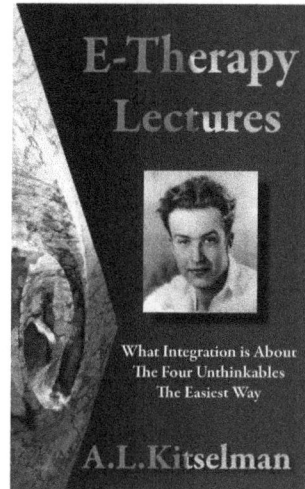

Would you like to ..

Improve your conduct? Is there a habit you'd like to get rid of?

Experience extreme physical pleasure? Intense, ever-fresh happiness? Deep impartial calmness?

Lose the feeling of insecurity? Make an end of doubt and perplexity? Lose all sense of fear, hatred, and grief?

Become a prodigy in science, government, business, art or education? A genius in originality, mental grasp, or in understanding others? Would you like to develop supernormal powers?

Become fully integrated? To be directly aware of things (without needing to sense them or think about them)? To realize a state of being in which there is no obstruction?

These pages tell how.

From Masterworks International Publishing
ISBN: 978-0-9565803-7-5

Also available:

E-Therapy Lectures: What Integration is About, The Four Unthinkables and The Easiest Way.
From Masterworks International Publishing
ISBN: 978-0-9565803-8-2